MW01120151

HOW DO THEY MAKE THAT?

ICE CREAM

Jan Bernard and John Willis

Go to **www.av2books.com**, and enter this book's unique code.

BOOK CODE

Q 9 4 3 4 5 9

AV² by Weigl brings you media enhanced books that support active learning.

AV² provides enriched content that supplements and complements this book. Weigl's AV² books strive to create inspired learning and engage young minds in a total learning experience.

Your AV² Media Enhanced books come alive with...

Audio
Listen to sections of the book read aloud.

Key Words
Study vocabulary, and complete a matching word activity.

Video
Watch informative video clips.

Quizzes
Test your knowledge.

Embedded Weblinks
Gain additional information for research.

Slide Show
View images and captions, and prepare a presentation.

Try This!
Complete activities and hands-on experiments.

... and much, much more!

Published by AV² by Weigl
350 5th Avenue, 59th Floor
New York, NY 10118
Website: www.av2books.com

Copyright © 2017 AV² by Weigl
All rights reserved. No part of this publication may be reproduced, stored in a retrieval system, or transmitted in any form or by any means, electronic, mechanical, photocopying, recording, or otherwise, without the prior written permission of the publisher.

Library of Congress Cataloging-in-Publication Data

Names: Bernard, Jan, author | and Willis, John, author.
Title: Ice cream / Jan Bernard.
Description: New York, NY : AV2 by Weigl, [2017] | Series: How do they make that? | Includes bibliographical references and index.
Identifiers: LCCN 2016005655 (print) | LCCN 2016006194 (ebook) | ISBN 9781489645333 (hard cover : alk. paper) | ISBN 9781489649997 (soft cover : alk. paper) | ISBN 9781489645340 (Multi-user ebk.)
Subjects: LCSH: Ice cream, ices, etc.--Juvenile literature. | Ice cream industry--Juvenile literature.
Classification: LCC TX795 .B469 2017 (print) | LCC TX795 (ebook) | DDC 637/.4--dc23
LC record available at http://lccn.loc.gov/2016005655

Printed in the United States of America in Brainerd, Minnesota
1 2 3 4 5 6 7 8 9 0 20 19 18 17 16

072016
210716

Project Coordinator: John Willis   Art Director: Terry Paulhus

Every reasonable effort has been made to trace ownership and to obtain permission to reprint copyright material. The publishers would be pleased to have any errors or omissions brought to their attention so that they may be corrected in subsequent printings.

Weigl acknowledges Getty Images, iStock, Newscom and Alamy as its primary image suppliers for this title.

Contents

Sweet Ice Cream

Yum! A sweet chocolate ice cream cone is the perfect treat on a hot day. How about a thick strawberry milkshake? Some kinds of ice cream have swirls and some have chunks. Do you like to pour caramel sauce on top, or do you prefer sprinkles and nuts? Ice cream is delicious however you like it.

Ice cream is a delicious dessert that comes in many flavors.

Have you thought about how ice cream is made? There are many steps in the process. The first step starts at a dairy farm. That is where cows spend their days eating grass, alfalfa, and corn. They use part of the energy they get from this food to make milk. That is important, because milk is the main **ingredient** in ice cream.

Dairy cows are the important first step of making ice cream.

Milk from the cows is the main ingredient in ice cream.

At the Dairy Farm

Dairy cows are milked every day. Farmers lead the cows into milking stalls. A milking machine is hooked up to their udders to take the milk. A single cow can give about 55 to 60 pounds (25 to 27 kilograms) of milk a day. Farmers are paid by the pound for milk and not by the gallon.

A gallon of milk weighs about 8.5 pounds (4 kg).

These trucks not only take milk from the dairy and bring it to the ice cream factory, they also keep the milk cold.

Milk is warm when it comes out of a cow. The milk is quickly put into milk holding tanks. This keeps it from spoiling. These tanks are like your refrigerator at home, only much bigger. Every few days, a refrigerated **tanker truck** visits the dairy farm. The milk in the holding tanks is piped into the tanker truck. The truck then takes the milk to its next stop, the ice cream factory.

An Ice Cream Factory

Once the milk arrives at the factory, it is tested. The tests show if the milk is fresh and safe. Workers also see how much butterfat is in the milk. Butterfat is another name for cream. Milk comes from different dairies. The milk is mixed together and stored in large cold storage bins. Next, the milk is separated into cream and **skimmed** milk.

Now, it is time to make the basic ice cream mix. A worker uses a very large blender to mix together the main ingredients.

Milk and cream are kept in large tanks. The tanks keep the milk cool until it is ready for the next step.

What are those ingredients? They are cream, skimmed milk, sweeteners, and **stabilizers.**

Cream is a very important part of the ice cream mix. More cream makes ice cream taste good. It also makes ice cream smoother and thicker. Adding more cream also makes the ice cream cost more.

Skimmed milk makes ice cream good for you. It has protein, calcium, vitamins, and minerals that your body needs.

Sweeteners give ice cream a sweet taste. Cane sugar or beet sugar are often used. So are corn sweeteners and even honey.

All of the ice cream ingredients are mixed together before adding any special flavors.

Stabilizers come from different parts of plants. They are used in very small amounts. They keep **ice crystals** from forming in the ice cream. When ice crystals form in ice cream it can feel sandy or gritty in your mouth. You do not want that.

These main ingredients make the ice cream mix. It only needs to blend for a few minutes. Once that is done, it is time for the next step.

Next, two important things happen to the mix. It is **pasteurized** and **homogenized**. When the mix is pasteurized, it is heated. This kills **bacteria** in the mix.

Raw milk is milk as it comes right out of the cow. It can make people sick, because it contains bacteria.

Pasteurization keeps ice cream safe. The process makes sure things that can make people sick don't get into the ice cream.

Bacteria are very tiny living things. They are all around us all the time. We need some kinds of bacteria to keep us healthy. Good bacteria help us digest our food better. However, some bacteria can make us very sick. That is the kind of bacteria that is sometimes found in raw milk. The mix is heated to 161° Fahrenheit (72° Celsius) for 15 seconds. That is all it takes. The bacteria in the ice cream will be gone.

Homogenization is the next step. Cream often separates from other ingredients. To stop this, the cream is broken into very tiny bits. This makes the cream stay mixed with the other ingredients. That is exactly what ice cream makers want. A large machine called a homogenizer is used. The ice cream mix is shot into the homogenizer with high pressure. The pressure breaks up the cream. After the mix is homogenized, it is cooled quickly. Then, it sits for four hours or more.

Special machines are used to make sure ice cream stays mixed together and does not separate.

Coloring can also be added to the flavor vats.

Yummy Flavors

Why do we eat ice cream? We love the flavors. That means the next step is really important. At this point the mix does not have much flavor. It is mostly just sweet milk and cream. When the mix goes into large flavor vats, different flavors are added. Some ice cream will become vanilla. Some ice cream will become chocolate. Some other flavors that can be added include peach, peppermint, and strawberry.

The mixture is then pumped into a large mixing freezer. Inside the freezer, blades turn while air is added to the mix. Adding air is important. Without some air mixed in, your ice cream would be as hard as an ice cube.

Cookie dough, cookies and cream, and praline are just some of the flavors that need chunks added to them.

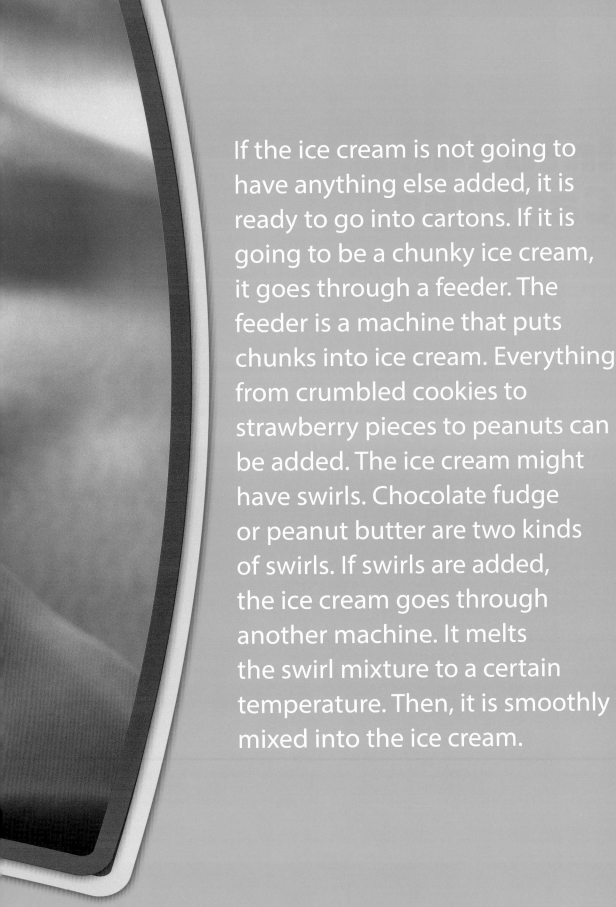

If the ice cream is not going to have anything else added, it is ready to go into cartons. If it is going to be a chunky ice cream, it goes through a feeder. The feeder is a machine that puts chunks into ice cream. Everything from crumbled cookies to strawberry pieces to peanuts can be added. The ice cream might have swirls. Chocolate fudge or peanut butter are two kinds of swirls. If swirls are added, the ice cream goes through another machine. It melts the swirl mixture to a certain temperature. Then, it is smoothly mixed into the ice cream.

Into the Cartons

Now, it is time to fill the cartons. Machines called fillers quickly fill cartons with ice cream as they move along a **conveyor belt**. Next, a machine puts a lid on each of the cartons. Finally, the cartons pass under an ink jet. It prints the date the ice cream **expires** onto each carton.

The ice cream is not ready to leave the factory. It now has to be hardened. That means it has to be frozen solid. Then, the ice cream is less likely to melt during shipment. The cartons are put into a spiral hardener.

Once all of the fillings are included in the ice cream, the ice cream cartons are filled.

A spiral hardener is a freezing machine that can be a tall as a two-story building. It has a conveyor belt that spirals upward through the machine. As the cartons go up, fans blast cold air. When the cartons come out, they are frozen solid.

Next, ice cream cartons need to be packaged. They are bundled together by flavor and wrapped in plastic for shipping. The ice cream packages are called sleeves. The sleeves are then packed on large pallets.

Ice cream batches must be tasted before leaving the factory. Random cartons are also tested to make sure the ice cream is safe to eat.

As the cartons move up the spiral hardener, they get colder and colder until frozen solid.

Ice cream can be found in the freezer section of most local grocery stores.

Into Your Bowl

When a batch of ice cream passes its tests, the ice cream cartons can be shipped. The pallets are loaded onto refrigerated trucks. Then, they are shipped to your grocery store. Check out all the choices you have. Will you choose rocky road or butter pecan? How about vanilla fudge ripple? You can choose one that is extra creamy, or you can try one that is low in fat. There are a lot of delicious choices to make when picking ice cream.

Pick your favorite. Then, stick it in your freezer at home. For your next treat, grab a big bowl, scoop in some ice cream, and add some toppings. That is all you need to make a big ice cream sundae. Grab a spoon and dig in.

Quiz

Match the steps with the pictures.

A. Dairy farm

B. Make ice cream mix

C. Mix in flavors

D. Put into cartons

E. Ship to grocery stores

Answers
1.B 2.E 3.D 4.A 5.C

Key Words

bacteria: small living things that are harmful or helpful

conveyor belt: a moving belt that takes materials from one place to another in a factory

expires: when something reaches the end of the time it can be used

homogenized: when cream is broken into small bits and spread evenly in liquid

ice crystals: a solid form of water that can be sandy in ice cream

ingredient: something that is added to a mixture, such as one item in a recipe list

pasteurized: when food is heated to a high temperature and harmful bacteria is killed

skimmed: milk that has had the cream removed

stabilizers: ingredients that stop ice crystals from forming in ice cream

tanker truck: a truck that is used to move liquids or gasses from one place to another

Index

Log on to www.av2books.com

AV² by Weigl brings you media enhanced books that support active learning. Go to www.av2books.com, and enter the special code found on page 2 of this book. You will gain access to enriched and enhanced content that supplements and complements this book. Content includes video, audio, weblinks, quizzes, a slide show, and activities.

AV² Online Navigation

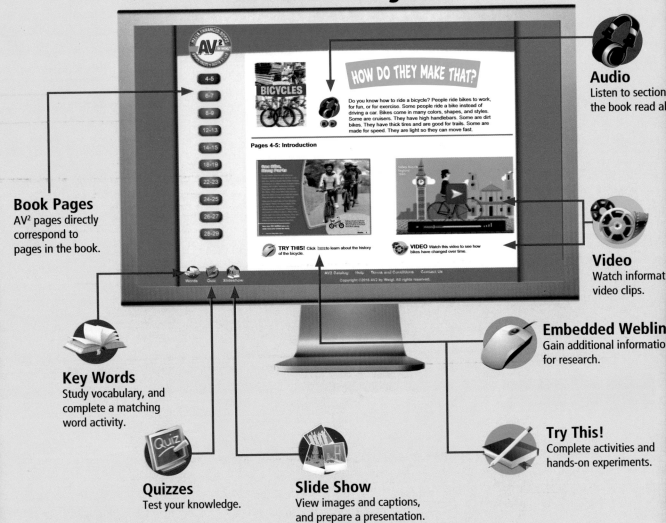

Audio
Listen to section
the book read al

Book Pages
AV² pages directly
correspond to
pages in the book.

Video
Watch informat
video clips.

Key Words
Study vocabulary, and
complete a matching
word activity.

Embedded Weblin
Gain additional informatio
for research.

Try This!
Complete activities and
hands-on experiments.

Quizzes
Test your knowledge.

Slide Show
View images and captions,
and prepare a presentation.

AV² was built to bridge the gap between print and digital. We encourage you to tell us what you like and what you want to see in the future.

Sign up to be an AV² Ambassador at www.av2books.com/ambassador.

Due to the dynamic nature of the Internet, some of the URLs and activities provided as part of AV² by Weigl may have changed or ceased to exist. AV² by Weigl accepts no responsibility for any such changes. All media enhanced books are regularly monitored to update addresses and sites in a timely manner. Contact AV² by Weigl at 1-866-649-3445 or av2books@weigl.com with any questions, comments, or feedback.